Matters for You Alone

Matters for You Alone

Poems

Leslie Williams

SL /. NT
BOOKS

MATTERS FOR YOU ALONE
Poems

Slant Books
P.O. Box 60295
Seattle, WA 98160

www.slantbooks.org

Cataloguing-in-Publication data:

Names: Williams, Leslie

Title: Matters for you alone: poems / Leslie Williams

Description: Seattle, WA: Slant Books, 2024

Identifiers: ISBN 978-1-63982-166-2 (hardcover) | ISBN 978-1-63982-165-5 (paperback) |
   ISBN 978-1-63982-167-9 (ebook)

Subjects: LCSH: Poetry | American poetry--21st century | Friendship--Poetry | Christian poetry, American

Contents

for a friend
whose heart demands the infinite

Who breaks the thread, the one who pulls, the one who holds on?
—JAMES RICHARDSON, *APHORISMS*

MOONSTONE, TIGER'S EYE

It's called *chatoyance*, the gems' bands of reflected light.
Bright blinked streaks in metamorphic rock, rock
that makes up much of the earth's crust
here at the grassy boundary where I'm lying creaturely
as a shrew, pressing cheek to ground
at cat's-prowl level, watching
stalks come out and beaks go in.
Night hunters, I'll learn from you.
It's not like looking for arcane cave marks
or shadows on an ultrasound. What there is to know
is like the cool within stone
vaults, while outside summer's wrinkling through
the foothills' pleats, sunlight through the chinks.
I would creep closer. I would be less
about things and more inside them.

I

IF YOU PREFER NOT TO FILL OUT
THE VISITOR CARD

In the film loop at the entrance to the aquarium,
Jacques Cousteau tells of a dolphin in captivity
who, on the death of her companion, stubbornly
kept the corpse from sinking. I think about my body
and its flagging spirit, nudging it up for air.

Have you ever asked for glory? When Moses did,
God hid him in the cleft of a rock, covered him
with His hand and passed on by. When Moses came down
his face was shining fearfully such that he had to wear a veil.

There was one dolphin I grew attached to, came back often
to visit. His face, like he swallowed a canary. The perpetual smile
lost me in an ocean, another flesh, a tank. Stayed with me
in kindness I hadn't felt or given in a while.

As I entered the Sunday door, the woman in the denim shirt
clasped my hand, said *welcome.* Her eyes were lit with the greatest
greeting, as if for the sun itself. I had to turn and run
away, unable to stay a minute more. In a flash-burn instant
I became bearable, but then the kindness itself
became too much to bear.

PILGRIM CROSSING

I watched the well-washed women
in pearls and power suits stride
across the seaport, smashing
wet leaves underfoot, my own precious
hours jimmied loose and spiraling
away, the mountain looming
in the far off, sphinxlike.
I'd been harboring a home-dream,
the almost active hope. At salty bars
I'd belly up, listen to the locals talk,
see them laugh, and in the morning lie
so blithely, drinking up my breakfast—
unvarnished, crude, most true. I walked
down to Kinkos, put the letter—*dear
L.*—in the mail. Thin crust of snow
so crystalline it broke under my boots.
I didn't know to whom I was always
saying *sorry, sorry.* But now I do.

THE SPECK

I had never met a mind so perfectly
intoxicant, so redolent, so like a grove
of orange trees. Blossoms dazzling, but shaken
easily, maybe never to become fruit.

Some days our estrangement seems a simple case
of love cut down to fit
mature and separate realms, shaped by no-fault
circumstance, as way led on to way.

Other times I see my lips pressed hard in the judging look
we hated on our mothers, when boys brought home
did not remove their hats, nor ask to be excused.

If I try to see my friend from higher ground
she's wearing her fawn-colored coat outside the sorry
pizza place. Or sobbing under the bridge.

I see her waiting for the green line early, freshly
showered, starting again.
How she really tried. How she cannot help it.

PAPER LANTERNS BLOWING IN THE TREES

my friend was living hand
to hand down on the Ave
stepping off curb into gutter
river—up to the ankles
no getting around

out-
sider
status is
no status at
all

in the rain of unbelonging
thinking herself out of range
of the father who waits
lit as in the Rembrandt
arms outstretched

lit

the
text says
he'll see us
coming from far

what's lodged in us
we must recover or remove
like diving over and over
for the trinket on the bottom
of Ms. Drum's pool

                    the
                  lantern
             keeps return-
           ing as it burns
                   past

learning to swim with warm
water in her ear
or camp stove cooking
with a slender
flame

                    I'd

                  been
              thinking
           we should be
       friends then a wind
               came

for separate
candle-lit sedans
whisked us far
from youth's
recursive gleam

> our
> need for
> solitude
> its watery
> joy

AN EASIER HOSPITALITY

Too tired to find
the earrings, not bold enough
for lipstick, I'm not original, fearless, sanguine
as friend I now remember you

driving barefoot with dark painted toes,
speeding down hot empty roads
in an open Chevrolet,
your expert way of playing tambourine

on stage—you'd say
good girls, bad girls are loved the same,
but sometimes bad girls are loved more,
having come a further way.

It makes everything so splendid—splendid
and confused—what I've crept to
before sunup: wooden cradle, cup of milk,
to these I have belonged

entirely—it *was* love and *is*
love and I think it will always last.
But Sunday setting up the brunch and filling
coffee urns, I felt shifty,

like a salesgirl of the secondhand,
who holds the door then goes off
down the street alone,
once everyone is in.

IN THE SCROLL OF THE BOOK

If I could get my hands on it, I'd devour
her secret history, compare my fragrant

memories to see if some of ours agree.
Did she inscribe our breezing in

to burner neighborhoods with the poshest set,
fluttering fine camel coats for *tête-à-têtes*

in chill fall rain, spilled laughs to drown
the fetid streets, or cleanse? Do her entries

say how I spent mornings, holed up in stockrooms
nursing my double life? That I had to work while

she slept in? The worst is, sometimes she's a party
I'd want to crash again. What about the register

of befriending me, while outside her ex slashed
my tires on city street? And that she really changed

six times until the sweater matched her eyes
and the Bluebird cab she called. Is it true, to each

a judgment according to what's been given?
A guilty shimmer's gathering, about to break

over my head—and look, when I lean
closer, I see our names are written in the book,

both with question marks beside them.

VANISHING LAKE

My interior paramour—
when last we spoke
anything further was foolish
to say, having exhausted every
route, witnessing the ease
with which great fires
can be extinguished,
down to eating
just a little, surviving
in secret—what awes me
now: the brute naïveté
that powered us, lazing
in meandering streams until
they cut off to oxbows,
isolated ear-shaped lakes—
but then I felt the swell
of an emergency, and only
one of us could swim.

THE AMULET

Mergansers and the mirrored pines in ponds remember
my friend as friendly, but also always
jockeying for better offers.

Pathetic how long I hung around
waiting for her to do a flyover
like a Blue Angel in tight formation above

the stadium bowl, where I alone was satisfied with beer
and Polish sausage happy-shouts, the comfort
of anyone in the crowd feeling glad—

meanwhile the haggard firs
may not make it through the deep clean
of the neighborhood as it turns over, keeping only

what it needs—ranch-style houses being razed
in a rage for something new—I feel it too
in my fifties kitchen with the hebetude—

but lakes persist with ducks
of my discovering how much I hate it
when people skirt so blithely

with their little blasphemies,
never acknowledging what is to me
my God so deadly serious.

That long gloomy spring a cavern
opened beneath her tenacious trading up,
so I packed out what belonged to me, plus

a Marian blue oval rescued from a broken
bracelet on her basement windowsill,
and carry still.

AS SEEN IN FRESCOES NOW EFFACED

At the seashore a boy holds a clamshell
beside a small hole in the sand.

St. Augustine in purple robes paces the beach—
How can it be? Three in one. One in three.

Can't you see? the boy says. *I'm using this shell*
to scoop the whole sea into this pool—

*You can't do that—*Augustine insists.

Child: *I will sooner empty the sea into this pool*
than you will manage the mystery of the Trinity.

The boy (some say an angel) disappears.

When a group of hermit crabs
encounters a large empty shell

they assemble in a line in order of size
for each to cast off its pinched dwelling

and slip into the next more spacious
home. Quickly, before exposed

fragile bodies cook in tropical sun,
or get washed away by rogue waves.

∽

We're taught to love
by someone—a series of them—

each seeking a brief shelter
as the spirit searches
for more capacious

seas—*O give me*
continence and chastity O

Lord not yet—

PROVED BY THE SPARROW

I stay up all night to hear the whole story,
race for the 9 a.m. train. At work I burn
through love song, elegy, song the earbuds repeat.

Let's just say this about that. What's love? Right now
life is closing down, all the curtains and doors,
like a seasonal cottage shuttered for winter.

What's the commandment? In this part of life
I walk over bare floor to window, see love
taxi forever away. The future must be foreordained,

proved by the sparrow flying over
with a cricket in its beak, dropping it
on the fire escape. All the lines in my palm

have a firmament. All household gods have a niche,
and a more beautiful empty shrine is kept
for the Unknown God, the most compassionate,

the one who knows my coming in and going
out, the one I fear the most. More and more I feel
threaded by the divine in life, and what a fine needle it is.

FIRST-CLASS RELICS

Ground to a cinder might describe
my younger self,
or *wearing a garment*

of skins—smoking
outside the wedding hall,
always the girl

who brought the toaster,
sorry to California
for how ordinary I was

and readily corruptible,
drinking from any
offered cup.

But my friend
could absolutely
martyr it

and yet next morning
preserve an air
of isolation, herself still

veiled and precious,
carried high
above adoring crowds.

FRIEND SHIFT

I'm trying to forgive my friend
who arrives like a bleeder
in an ambulance.

I should minimize
exposure, as to a bad
virus or too much sun.

I'm always the shadow,
the "local talent," sweeping
the floor, fêting her

even when my new baby
had just come home.
I was gulping

cranberry ginger ales
in dazed thirst to restore
myself as she uncorked

another dark-green bottle,
put her thumb
in the deep punt

of the heavy bell-shaped
bottom, and poured herself
more red.

FINE PRINT

A biker in the checkout line has cursive
on his arm: *He has removed our sins as far from us*

as the west is from the east. In purple ink. His skin's
like parchment from a calf's cleaned hide: soaked,

dried, stretched, then scraped with a crescent-
shaped knife. Treated with lime to make it accept

the writing. All my nights are like papyrus,
drenched in tears, a wash of disobedience

staining my blank ease. How craven,
wretched, wasteful I've been, trusting the sad

needs of flesh, endangering the small animal
of spirit. And yet, a hungry lion

on the veld will prowl elsewhere
if the wind might shift. Save my skin, O wind.

TEACH US TO NUMBER OUR DAYS

I keep asking to be un-flattened, resuscitant—

for it's unseemly to lie abed
when every possible blessing's near.

Children, to care for them,

their secret rooms
of pushpin maps, clay castles, shoes—

taking stock can save a thing so I'm lost
in doing that, may not come back.

Half-painted canvases, peach pit, books—
melodic through the door half-cracked,

same as music from my own old room
and the shoebox with the ashes

of three small dogs, a bottle
of Jack Daniels, and the afternoons

I went looking for a suitable face
with which to persevere.

MUSEUM OF ADULT LIFE

sometimes
feel best removed
from floor display
stored climate safe
and buffer-wrapped
in archival tissue
like a fine small-
shouldered jar

TIDAL MOUTH

Sadness lies lord of my whole inner length:
a dead-weight twin who makes no sound.
There's something to love in her dumb strength,

but I'm ready for relief, on the brink
in August heat after a sweltering round
with this sadness: lies, my whole inner length.

Fresh water streams into marsh-inked
damp; slashing through reeds I drag us both down.
There's something to love in the dumb strength

of breath, inhaling low odors of green as we sink
in dank hammocks of moss. Here I long to drown
the sadness lying down my whole inner length.

In muddied sand I find a furrow shell—wings
unhinged, bereft of its soft architect, outgrown.
There's something to love in the dumb strength

of relics, salted away by an ocean's sting.
I'd be hollow and haunted as a shell without
my sadness, lying lord my whole inner length.
There's too much to love in its dumb strength.

SUNSET 4:14

Time to shuffle around again and pull down all the blinds.
Tomorrow morning it will be the present moment. Gaze
on static driveway (snowbird neighbors six months and a day
away), the one Japanese maple furiously red,
highly perishable, no doubt flammable. (Why is *in-*
flammable painted on gas-tanker trucks hurtling down
the highway? Why must everything confuse?) We must put on
imperishability as Paul says, be clothed with new
life. What you sow is not the body that will be, only
a seed. When you arrive, it might be a wintry coastal
inn (soft chairs and piles of blankets, a wide fireplace). It's in
remotest outpost where the welcome feels most intimate.
A lone caretaker keeps lamps trimmed and lit, knows how you like
your tea. As salt is known (completely) by the unknown sea.

MOTHER DREAM WITH SUMMER AND WINTER

Children's seashore voices tumbling with surf,
long-tailed kites high above the strand, tanned bodies
taken home to nap in tufted beds.

I went out walking then left the road
with no map for where to go—
so around the snowed-over baseball field, stopping

to pull off my boots and socks and thrust bare feet
through slick ice crust into soft confectionary
snow below—the nerves radiating a victorious, shocked

brilliance—then a helicopter flew over, its dun underside
exactly like a moon crab's articulated abdomen—and
it sighted me.

& THEN A WIND CAME

Spring lonesome but also dreading
    summer's crush of merrymaking, I return
        (amid the cloudbursts) to Mt. Auburn's
            visible small markers (grave &
                tree I mean), seeking

    luscious sapwood centers to what's trying
        to be felled—& asking to be seen
            with druid eyes—to fuzz the time
                between right now & earlier states
                    of kingdom, smudging lines around
                      the creaturely to let in more

                    of what's beside—it's how I know
              You care for me, by trees, by fruit come
        down to leaf, by leading me on old routes
    to this new day in which I've never been so
lonesome, crushed before the May—

LOVE IS THE CROOKED THING

Little brown dove, is that you?
You're a model for the core of me.
Picking up the twig, dropping it three times.

Trying to get a burst again of what it's like to feel alive,
watching for the fox,
might she be put forward to be seen.

Burnish-fur, black socks, stealth, composure, all!
How carefully we're made
of curiosity plus silence

so the marvelous might enter in.
Think of unnumbered atoms floating inside a stone.
And the relief in apprehending

we don't make ourselves.
Even the skink in crabapple tree,
even the mountains breaking into rocks

on their way to becoming
finest sand. All this, and what I could never see
was any space between us.

CONDOLENCE NOTE

When I felt friendship unraveling I clung to consolations—
small pine trees printed on my boys' sleeping bags, the bright sugar
on hard surfaces of scones—for the shadowy way they conjured
the lake of our ease, nodding to love's nimbus. I was saying goodbye
not knowing it, driving around to the pick-up lane for a huge fiddle-leaf
fig like the one in my friend's living room, but it would not fit in the passenger
seat. I started weeping as if the stranger in the orange apron should also grieve.

VESPERS

As our party readied the boat
my friend stood on the dock alone
wearing the sandals she hated, an impulse splurge
that had briefly made her feel funky, friendly, able
to compete—but now she had to pay for half of her child's shrink.

She said *thanks, but no thanks*
when I invited her to join, as if prayer were an exotic food
she might be allergic to, or didn't trust
she had the palate for, didn't trust herself.
Sorry, it's not for me, she called as we shoved off, gathered speed.

IN THE MAIN

Beaten down and wayward as the windhowl,
like my bare colossal unpruned trees

I cracked and groaned all night. I should call
right now, take care of things

(it's up to me), but from dark gray deep
the morning has become spectacularly calm

and sunny now, the sky a mainsail blue.
It's been so long since I've seen sky like this.

I almost turn from it
because I know it not to last, that by tonight

it will be cold and sealed
for snow again. But shouldn't I try to bask a bit, take

whatever sun my eyes can get? I've burned the lamps
till retinas blazed; I've been that mother

driving carpool, mending hats, collecting
bottles and the patchwork cats;

I have lived a thousand lives today in one
and I have waited long

for sun or sleep or for my boys to come on home,
so OK, sun, now you can go; I've steeled

myself, done war against, have not allowed
my face to fall in face of

faithlessness, not at all, my dear commitments, but
the cleaning up or making calls or getting snacks, today

I've put them off—I'll likely die without the doorknob fixed
that rattles in the hall—I'm hungry, tired, dis-

satisfied, or *too.* I've been wearing
only one pair of my shoes. I can get to rooms in me

where I don't care, shut them off
and be no more dangerous.

GENTLY USED

As happened on the Easter Vigil, I bestowed
a shepherd from a thrifted
crèche, which I gave her piece by piece
each year until she held the very baby.
Did we drift because she left the church?
Or was it my own hurt that carried me,
little boat, away—

BLURRED EDGE

I cannot rest with her face looking
from the book jacket, an acquired

harrowing that transmits
chronic disorder seen—shattered

plays, the Chinatowns, fractional
recoveries, fever qualities

palpable but early, as entanglements
beginning to form far off—

what attracted her enough
to make a fateful stop for?

Why do I get to break lobsters clean
inside a restaurant, when years down

on Telegraph I'd known the same ravening
for whatever calamity would have me,

not finding the hidden entry to my own
life, lit like a paper lantern yet

in danger. Runaway afternoons circling
her worlds—shiny masks, a Mardi Gras

among the poverties, maquillage, susurrus
and green diamonds, boys of summer

spinning across the innocence left—
I long for her return, unscarred

and plain, a window
without need of arch, for her to be

the one who slept while trains
rattled somewhere else.

DREAM WITH WINNOWING FORK

One ski weekend last year there was thundersnow, high wind—but
we had all arrived inside after a good day on the mountain: eating,
laughing, warmed by the lodge's fire. The storm seemed contained,
though the sky still flashed behind a layer of cloud. My friend
decided to take her children out on the patio to dine in better
atmosphere, under a heated awning with votives all aglow. We went on
with our meal inside and then came a rattling explosion; I ran to look
out the French doors: not a soul in sight. As if snow had been
falling peacefully for hours, it draped everything. I could see
the spaces between whitened planks of the deck's floor and between
smaller slats of wooden tables, but no sign of life, nor
anything I had known to be there just minutes before. Not a broken
plate or crumb, not the smallest disturbance of snow.

SHAKE THE DUST

the whole library blown through
doors standing open
and every book

at the party I was the lone
cold adult outside minding kids
on trampoline though no one
asked me to

I couldn't stand not being there
to protect or intervene
while other mothers
drank festively inside

the difference undid me finally
I should be less martyrish
though some things aren't related
to our mistakes

my friend decided God was not
enough for her
it was more the universe
she trusted in

VEIL TORN IN TWO

A cottontail has settled in the yard, eyes lifted
amid foraging, to regard and be regarded.

And the orange fox last night, sighted like a lantern
in the open place, face smeared white like paint.

The third an owl, flying in from medicine wheel
to flank the desktop's sacred deer

deftly sculpted out of kindergarten clay.
More animals of the book, like us.

Then a seraph with a pair of tongs
takes a live coal from the altar, touches it

to my lips. *Who will go for us?*
I've heard that on Atonement Day one celebrant

wore bells, lashed a rope around his waist
before entering the high holy place. If the jingling

stopped, the other priests would know
the divine had been too bright to gaze on

and so to pull their end of rope, until their friend's
corpse came sliding out from behind the curtain.

II

DREAM OF BEING ALIVE

Because we most love what we best lose
ourselves in, let's pull on sweaters, enter
the story again. The cashmere I choose
has been lifted from a hundred winter
goats, fine fleece combed in spring
from their undercoats. But *unwell* soaks
through, overflows rooms and lingers
in the house's good bones, cloaked
behind walls as I try to work or sleep,
dress or use the telephone. Despair
can move as water, light, or air, to steep
and shallow places equally, and anywhere.
Poor goats. Their lost wool held
so close against shivering selves.

NINETY-NINE STORIES OF LOVE

I thought my God
was a gentle hen for hiding me
but here she is
ruffling out my failings
in lurid pops of lapis blue.

I'm loved
like the defrocked priest
who, after converting thousands
in the convention hall,
got hammered alone in a hotel room.

A downed robin egg's on garden edge
the same day my son is leaving—
it bears the crack of *watch him fly*
as he wheels his silver car
out of the drive.

Pathless meadow, I've fallen
but awakened
from every sleep thus far.
In the after-grass
of crashing rains, hot sun sprawls

across my body like large hands,
and tender ramps spring up
oniony and wild,
but only for a week.
Always glutton me to these.

Down by the waterline, being
on the breeze,
watching and wondering
as others played
I kind of felt so fleet.

In my little room
before the cloister is entire
it must be the world
is glory; glory we lie down to,
unite in and untie.

To live very quietly
I saw as one of my strengths—
pocketing a grooved shell
proximate
to the work of prayer

to taking flight above the shoals
where sharks roll
feeding in the scrum,
an aerial endless view of ocean
till the god of the seas says

—child—
even
as bitterns
course the barrens
there

QUARTZES FORMED IN HIDDEN CHAMBERS

Riots of passionate gist, pink light
on frozen pavement and the combustible soul
we watch dissipate and re-form—now when everyone's
safe in bed I feel a different rage (for things to stay the same)
but rafts are always leaving and we have to scrabble on, still
thirsty for the kind of love that takes it out of our very hides,
aware that   Deep Siberian   only perilous
extremes   purple glister   will yield
geodes cracking   amethyst crystals   to reveal
it takes years in billions   a stunning pressure
to make a gem's small blast of being—it's by and
with and in divine provision that we dwell
amidst the always-moving hills.

PILGRIM BRIDGE

Impassable divide
human—divine

Your vision and mine
concur very partially

we both stare at disaster maps
but I need

to lie down
what's the right way

to sift among the seismic
where my friend lives

as one unified being
both flamboyant

and meek—
when tsunamis swept her

life so graveldown
every day was nothing

more than keeping head above
the scroll

when she showed me her bed
wrapped in weeds

I thought no one
could go on lying there

I thought why
that someone has to be me.

I'D BE IN RIGHT RELATION WITH THE WINE

and with answering the telephone. With asparagus and cantaloupe.
And what about my attitude toward high-heeled boots, the Revised
Prayer Book, the selfish friend?

With the sea I am all right, and, I think, my God.
I'm OK with wheat fields and this one hour of my time.

I'm not sure how I stand with the grass under unraked leaves
or with neighbors who complained about the party noise,
not sure about the owner of the dented car
for whom I did not leave a note.

What about the people in line behind me at the grocery store
while the bagger showed me pictures of her daughter's prom dress,
dark plum with lighter trim?

Where are they now, the kids I under-chaperoned while picking apples,
or the man who did not harm me when I was young,
though he could have, easily.
What if I wanted to make amends, to thank him?

I'm still not sure of my relationship with yoga,
or with the library to which I never returned the cassettes.

And what about the heirlooms I ignore, my unsightly spider veins,
the stiffed landlord, the exiled pet, the rebuffed visitor
from Uganda, the working poor I pass each day on the way to Peet's?

What about my unused eggs, the fired babysitter, the outstanding
invitation, the Uber driver I'd like to change my rating for, the nurse
I shouted at, the shriveled contact lens?

I'd like to be on clearest terms with everything as I am with silence
and my knockout roses, the line of linden trees.

FRIEND WITH ONIONSKIN

Dear L.—please tell me
how we go about it, under spell
of lone pine, whippoorwill,
chalice, bells—at nightfall time's
run out again, or sleep
has chosen me—listen, when
I scissored your note open a kind
of knock-off Northern California grace
came flooding in, striking
dishes, tablecloth, the spiky aster
in a hand-blown vase, binding
with a force so gravitational
it governed everything. Airmail
tissue bearing multitudes,
the thinnest places helpless
against light getting through.

SILENT RETREAT

March, Edgartown

I let myself out through the back gate
carrying a bag of garbage and my travel mug,
uneaten peanut butter, clementines, and rice cakes
after sweeping and turning off all the lights.
I left books wrapped in tissue on the quiet kitchen
counter, untouched pressed pages with luscious
covers of freckled peaches and engraved beakers
in hammered silver. I left early because more snow
was coming, got up hurriedly from the chair
to make the last ferry. How many storms
would rage, subside, and rage again before
the absent owner returned to find my thank-you gifts?
When would I be opened? The door fell closed
on a clean sea of marble, as if I'd been expelled.

LOVE (3)

A lamp is burning in an apartment window,
and strings of Christmas lights at 6:30 in the morning: a view
worthwhile for framing you, my someone *x* inside
simpatico, valorous, keen—most compassionate
to (I'm not proud of) my early catastrophic
openness, Constantinople and Trafalgar and all the jangled
hopes untamed—crowds invited up above the traffic noise,
street-lit rain-slick nights, an almost empty fridge—O dizzying
vivacities too costly to sustain! You say *here, come lay your head*
and so renounce the squelching voice that spiraled
through my girlhood: *it only matters that you "turn out all right,"*
as if a life is nothing more than a presentable
but tasteless cake.

                  Love, You want for me

                               a Jubilee, the flaming—

SOME OTHER BLAZE IN US

Here's what keeps me in it: cool Saturday
in fall, noticing a football practice across
the parking lot as I step out of my car, beside
the chain-link fence that's trapped a sheet
of gift wrap—shiny red mylar escaped
from someone's last-year Christmas trash—saved
there weathering the seasons, maybe belonged
to the family now going in the donut shop,
mom dressed neatly, hair brushed back, girls
still in pajamas. A little smoke puffs out
the stack at Waltham High; a whistle
sounds in bursts as boys run up the hill,
their helmets and jerseys red like the scrap
caught in the fence; now a man is holding
the Dunkin' door for a lady with a cane
who says *this door's so heavy;* he says *I know,
I had trouble with it too.* A fall weekend
will show up like a mountaintop, send
everything slipping into new range—time
to batten down, to look in the brown cup,
trees frosted early a few morning
hours. Of course I never have been
satisfied, but being here among the ready
leaves feels like a chaplaincy, come alongside
a world changing when it has no choice.

QUANTUM ENTANGLEMENT

A gang of turkeys has colonized the park.
Ugh! the big unbalanced
bodies and skinny necks. Wattles, caruncles, snoods.
Now a spurred-shank jenny
goes fancy-footing by, as if across parade grounds
where wonders may appear, in the majesty
of every ugly thing turning
beautiful, the way anything loved will be.
Which reminds me again
of L.—this morning in the mirror
a mote in my eye
I was trying to remove
and I thought: *definitely,* her faults
I grow painfully aware
amount to a speck compared
to those same mountains in me,
so I've lately grown obsessed
with physics: force and action, spooky action
at a distance, and love. Always
love. You can't see it
but what it makes you do is real.

CANTICLE WITH LOVE ENTIRE ITS SHAPE

Making a second cup of coffee
after taking the boys to school

I catch my own reflection
in the kettle's silver face,

sunlit window, shadowed
crossbars behind my head—I'm

an anchoress—whose mother nights
of offices and drudgery, lonely

terror of the fevers, every
cavil and constraint—are in a blaze

made known to me as greatest
privilege and grace,

all the care poured in
to raising them

returns to me full
measure, pressed down, shaken, running

over, by ephahs ten- and twenty-, hundred-
fold—overflowing
in hermetic morning.

STAR-DOGGED MOON

Here are days
that define and deify,

highways spanning out
like taffy or hot glass.

Do you remember me?

In me a beautiful little something loose
the way an engine part is.

I love—adore—a sight for sore eyes,
the prodigal friend returned, a feast,

rolling back carpets for dancing
toward morning on time's bare floor until

it's yielding all we've searched for,
not from afar where we had always looked,

but at most interior nanoscale,
closing every mental loop,

claiming each as intimate moon,
renaming lava plains as seas

of Tranquility, Serenity—
planting more and more flags

until the whole is taken
into vital astonishment of *here,*

the morning apartment swept,
the determined scent of transit.

ON SEEING OLD SKIS IN THE GARAGE

So many slopes they touched, and once
leaned outside while I tromped into the parlor
of an alpine monastery, clattering boots, my bluster
welcomed to dine silently with the brothers
who had also vowed to get to the powder
of what is daily fused with life: to glide, to carve,
to schuss and float with what the spirit clamors for—
even though my body's sluggish, slow, it remembers
mountains, glory in the snowfell
hill, its bluebell kindred skills—a rough *jouissance*
is what I brought, in all my choices good
and not so good, the might-have-beens
and new offerings from the range
I'm entering, something milder—I'd still strive
for the milk of kindness, hold out my simmering
so the fat might rise like broken proteins
to the top, to be skimmed off.

VIA NEGATIVA

You know about the longing to be made new,
to shuck the kind veneer and zeal to be a part
of things and instead to burrow in, concede the fears
of early-onset, spark-showering harm, fuses
blown like an old TV: alone watching
basketball in the days of knee socks when
hints rushed by in winter flurry, as Venus
and the sickle moon show then hide then show
themselves season after season, without which
this minute can't exist. You know everything
will come to be spit out, especially the histories
that thrilled and mattered most, none of this a big deal
by itself, like the unpaved road you drove
for the umpteenth time today when nails sank deep
in the tires, and what that represents.

BEGINNER LANDSCAPE

The sheep come back,
their faces
clean among the fold

brushed in stumbling
strokes till it's yourself
you see—

hip-hollowed,
limping with
old injuries,

moving toward
a brilliance in no way
commensurate,

halfway to the shrine
with crutches
torn away,

spirit fluttery as the iris
that yes, will need dividing—
wild burgundy, yellow, cream.

CONNECTIVE TISSUE

What's next for you? my teacher asks
as the new decade blooms. I'm learning
how to work silk yarn on the loom, lovely
instrument, stringed like the harp in sunlit
lobby outside the hospital chapel
where I ducked in yesterday to light a candle,
red votive for my friend who's been sneaking
off to radiation without telling
anyone. I'd like to stand tall instead
of collapsing into rag doll, into *wait*
and see. When I was younger I kept reading
a man is just a reed, but he's a thinking
reed. And she's the body, bruising easily
as sea grass in the salt marsh, played
by every current sweeping through.

IN TRUTH

We always cared to stray beyond the painted
restaurant doors—*Scottish Pub* or *Belgian Bistro*
high-gloss or *Classic Phone Box Red*—

and at the clinic we had ministered to strangers
as they guttered down to pools of wax, unable to scrape
themselves together again, so I got angry

at San Francisco lying quietly on the table,
empty rooms across the city, mad at the girl
who put flowers in a vase before they opened—

when dining out I'd grow impatient to excuse myself,
sneak down wrought-iron stairs and spy into the kitchen,
the station chefs so focused they forgot themselves.

It was my hunger for oblivion, its ten thousand shades
and flavors, that kept me, scorched me there—flattering,
really, so rarely is there anything that flints—

it has mostly left me now, but that was some rough hand
wrapped around my mouth, waking up this morning
with rain constant on the roof. I only know that through the fire
I'd want to talk to you again.

ON THE SIXTH DAY

Bats fly from cave mouth ultrasonically devout—

as kids will burst out for recess

through double-green doors flung wide—

and earthworms feel new cattle moving overhead

(each beast with unique rococo worlds inside)

you might call it a *petite musique*

you might know every daughter

has a different understanding of the father,

and a child will feel her molten vast identity

(never lonely but as liquid)

congruent with the particles and waves

of the first day's light—

HIDDEN ENTRY

Look for me in fields of hospice-heather, thistledown, bold
skeleton & cotton dress, pomegranates hem-stitched, begotten
fleece—unassisted woolly scene, bittering
to abscond with morphine stream above the winter
landscape—here's Moses putting down
his arm, the dwelling place, the wrecking
ball, the shining thing I sought—you know I'm out here
mudlarking, skyfaring among the broad
contrails and recommitted to the cricket, my wild twin.

CLOAK OF KINDNESS

You will be taught matters which are for you alone.
A silence opens, yes indeed.
Before, I'd been capsized

in the riotous depths of my own
governance, too far from shore the voyage out
became. It was a rage-lipped hunger, neither

surprised nor satisfied. The constant
stretching of the soul to accommodate
greater and greater distances till

I was an afternoon,
scrolling through old photos so proving
of forgiveness—arm-in-arm

blowing down the road.
I'd say get behind the lilac,
honeysuckle, and the seas.

I see our names are shining things
on a great countenance today.

NOTES

"Paper Lanterns Blowing in the Trees" alludes to the Gospel of Thomas: "If you do not bring forth what is within you, what you do not bring forth will destroy you," and refers to Luke 15:11-32.

In "Vanishing Lake," *interior paramour* is borrowed from Wallace Stevens's "Final Soliloquy of the Interior Paramour."

"As Seen in Frescoes Now Effaced" quotes and draws from augnet.org.

"Proved by the Sparrow" refers to Acts 17:22-23.

"Fine Print" refers to Psalm 103.

"Teach us to number our days" is from Psalm 90:12.

"Sunset at 4:14" borrows from 1 Corinthians 15.

In "Love Is the Crooked Thing," the title is from Yeats's poem "Brown Penny." The apple tree and skink, and the phrase "what I couldn't see was any space or separation between me and all these things," are from Phyllis Tickle's *The Shaping of a Life: A Spiritual Landscape*.

"Blurred Edge" borrows from—and is in memory of—Lynda Hull.

"Veil Torn in Two" refers to Isaiah 6.

"Love (3)" takes its title and inspiration from the poem by George Herbert.

"Canticle with Love Entire its Shape" borrows from Luke 6:38.

In "Cloak of Kindness," *you will be taught matters which are for you alone* is from Jean Pierre de Caussade's *Abandonment to Divine Providence.*

ACKNOWLEDGMENTS

Thank you to the editors of the following publications where some of the poems in this book first appeared: *America, Anglican Theological Review, Arcturus, Arts & Letters, Broad River Review, Cave Wall, Commonweal, Dappled Things, Dogwood: A Journal of Poetry and Prose, The Drum, Ekstasis, Harpur Palate, Hunger Mountain, Iron Horse Literary Review, Kenyon Review, Liberties, Mississippi Review, Poetry East, poets.org, Redivider, River Styx, Smartish Pace, Southern Poetry Review, Sou'wester*, and *Tahoma Literary Review*.

To Gregory Wolfe and Slant Books: Gratitude! And heartfelt thanks to the readers who helped over the years as this book took shape: Jennifer Barber, Sandra Beasley, T. J. Beitelman, Brian Burt, Abigail Carroll, Amy Clark, Katie Ford, Kirun Kapur, Heather King, Carla Panciera, Paul Pastor, Mike Perrow, Beth Platow, Lynne Potts, Glenn Stowell, Kate Westhaver, Corrie Williamson, and Scott Withiam. Thank you, wonderful friends. Thank you, my dear family. Thank you, my amazing sons. Thank you, Jack Goldsmith, best and most.

This book is set in Bunyan Pro from Canada Type, designed by Bill Troop and Patrick Griffin as a synthesis of Bunyan, the last face Eric Gill designed in 1934, and Pilgrim, the machine face based on it, issued by British Linotype in the early 1950s.

This book was designed by Shannon Carter, Ian Creeger, and Gregory Wolfe. It was published in hardcover, paperback, and electronic formats by Slant Books, Seattle, Washington.

Cover art: Laura Lasworth, *Heirlooms,* 2016. 48 x 60 inches, oil on panel.

Printed in the USA
CPSIA information can be obtained
at www.ICGtesting.com
JSHW021200120524
62813JS00007B/21

9 781639 821655